Joe Miller's _JESTS_

OR, THE

WITS

VADE-MECUM.

BEING

A Collection of the most Brilliant JESTS; the Politest REPARTEES; the most Elegant BONS MOTS, and most pleasant short Stories in the _English_ Language.

First carefully collected in the Company, and many of them

transcribed from the Mouth of the Facetious GENTLEMAN, whose Name they bear; and now set forth and published by his lamentable Friend and former Companion, _Elijah Jenkins_, Esq;

Most Humbly INSCRIBED

To those CHOICE-SPIRITS _of the_ AGE,

Captain BODENS, Mr. ALEXANDER POPE, Mr. Professor LACY, Mr. Orator HENLEY, and JOB BAKER, the Kettle-Drummer.

LONDON:

Printed and Sold by T. READ, in _Dogwell-Court, White-Fryars, Fleet-Street_, MDCCXXXIX.

Transcriber's Note: Jest number 59 was omitted from the original text.

JOE MILLER's _JESTS_.

1. The Duke of _A----ll_, who says more good Things than any Body, being behind the Scenes the First Night of the _Beggar's Opera_, and meeting _Cibber_ there, well _Colley_, said he, how d'you like the _Beggar's Opera_? Why it makes one laugh, my Lord, answer'd he, on the Stage; but how will it do in print. O! very well, I'll answer for it, said the Duke, if you don't write a Preface to it.[1]

[1] See _Cibber's_ Preface to _Provok'd Husband_.

2. There being a very great Disturbance one Evening at _Drury-Lane_ Play-House, Mr. _Wilks_, coming upon the Stage to say something to

pacify the Audience, had an Orange thrown full at him, which he having took up, making a low Bow, this is no _Civil Orange_, I think, said he.

3. Mr. _H--rr--n_, one of the Commissioners of the Revenue in _Ireland_, being one Night in the Pit, at the Play-House in _Dublin_, _Monoca Gall_, the Orange Girl, famous for her Wit and her Assurance, striding over his Back, he popp'd his Hands under her Petticoats: Nay, Mr. Commissioner, said she, you'll find no Goods there but what have been fairly entered.

4. _Joe Miller_ sitting one day in the Window at the _Sun-Tavern_ in _Clare-Street_, a Fish Woman and her Maid passing by, the Woman cry'd, _Buy my Soals; buy my Maids_: Ah, you wicked old Creature, cry'd honest _Joe_, _What are you not content to sell your own Soul, but you must sell your Maid's too?_

5. When the Duke of _Ormond_ was young, and came first to Court, he happen'd to stand next my Lady _Dorchester_, one Evening in the Drawing-Room, who being but little upon the Reserve on most Occasions, let a Fart, upon which he look'd her full in the Face and laugh'd. What's the Matter, my Lord, said she: Oh! I heard it, Madam, reply'd

the Duke, you'll make a fine Courtier indeed, said she, if you mind every Thing you _hear_ in this Place.

6. A poor Man, who had a termagant Wife, after a long Dispute, in which she was resolved to have the last Word, told her, if she spoke one more _crooked_ Word, he'd beat her Brains out: Why then _Ram's Horns_, you Rogue, said she, if I die for't.

7. A Gentleman ask'd a Lady at _Tunbridge_, who had made a very large Acquaintance among the Beaus and pretty Fellows there, what she would do with them all. O! said she, they pass off like the Waters; and pray, Madam, reply'd the Gentleman do they all _pass_ the _same Way_?

8. An Hackney-Coachman, who was just set up, had heard that the Lawyers used to club their _Three-Pence_ a-piece, four of them, to go to _Westminster_, and being called by a Lawyer at _Temple-Bar_, who, with two others in their Gowns, got into his Coach, he was bid to drive to _Westminster-Hall_: but the Coachman still holding his Door open, as if he waited for more Company; one of the Gentlemen asked him, why he did not shut the Door and go on, the Fellow, scratching his Head, cry'd you

know, Master, my Fare's a Shilling, I can't go for _Nine-Pence_.

9. Two Free-thinking Authors proposed to a Bookseller, that was a little decayed in the World, that if he would print their Works they would _set him up_, and indeed they were as good as their Word, for in six Week's Time he was in the _Pillory_.

10. A Gentleman was saying one Day at the _Tilt-Yard_ Coffee-House, when it rained exceeding hard, that it put him in Mind of the General _Deluge_; Zoons, Sir, said an old Campaigner, who stood by, who's that? I have heard of all the _Generals_ in _Europe_ but him.

11. A certain Poet and Player, remarkable for his Impudence and Cowardice, happening many Years ago to have a Quarrel with Mr. _Powell_, another Player, received from him a smart Box of the Ear; a few Days after the Poetical Player having lost his Snuff-Box, and making strict Enquiry if any Body had seen his _Box_; what said another of the Buskin'd Wits, _that_ which _George Powell_ gave you t'other Night?

12. _Gun Jones_, who had made his Fortune himself from a mean

Beginning, happening to have some Words with a Person who had known him some Time, was asked by the other, how he could have the Impudence to give himself so many Airs to him, when he knew very well, that he remember'd him seven Years before with hardly a _Rag to his A--_. You lie, Sirrah, reply'd _Jones_, seven Years ago _I had nothing but Rags to my A--_.

13. Lord _R----_ having lost about fifty Pistoles, one Night, at the Gaming-Table in _Dublin_, some Friends condoling with him upon his ill Luck, Faith, said he, I am very well pleas'd at what I have done, for I have bit them, by G---- there is not one Pistole that don't want Six-Pence of Weight.

14. Mother _Needham_, about 25 Years age being much in Arrear with her Landlord for Rent, was warmly press'd by him for his Money, Dear Sir, said she, how can you be so pressing at this dead Time of the Year, in about six Weeks Time both the Par----, and the C--n--v--c--n will sit, and then Business will be so brisk, that I shall be able to pay ten Times the Sum.

15. A Lady being asked how she liked a Gentleman's Singing, who had a

very _stinking Breath_, the Words are good, said she, but the _Air_ is intolerable.

16. The late Mrs. _Oldfield_ being asked if she thought Sir _W. Y._ and Mrs. _H----n_, who had both stinking Breaths, were marry'd: I don't know, said she, whether they are marry'd; but I am sure there is a _Wedding_ between them.

17. A Gentleman saying something in Praise of Mrs. _G----ve_, who is, without Dispute, a good Player, tho' exceeding saucy and exceeding ugly; another said, her Face always put him in mind of _Mary-Bone Park_, being desired to explain himself, he said, it was vastly _rude_ and had not one Bit of _Pale_ about it.

18. A pragmatical young Fellow sitting at Table over-against the learned _John Scot_, asked him what difference there was between _Scot_ and _Sot_: _Just the Breadth of the Table_, answered the other.

19. Another Poet asked _Nat Lee_ if it was not easy to write like a _Madman_, as he did: No, answered _Nat_, but it is easy to write like a _Fool_ as you do.

20. _Colley_, who, notwithstanding his _Odes_, has now and then said a good Thing, being told one Night by the late Duke of _Wharton_, that he expected to see him _hang'd_ or _beggar'd_ very soon, by G--d, said the Laureat, if I had your Grace's _Politicks_ and _Morals_ you might expect _both_.

21. Sir _Thomas More_, for a long Time had only Daughters, his Wife earnestly praying that they may have a Boy, at last they had a _Boy_, who when he came to Man's Estate, proved but simple; _thou prayedst so long for a Boy_, said Sir _Thomas_ to his Wife, _that at last thou hast got one who will be a Boy as long as he lives_.

22. The same Gentleman, when Lord Chancellor being pressed by the Counsel of the Party, for a _longer day_ to perform a Decree, said, _Take St._ Barnaby's _Day, the longest in the Year_; which happened to be the next Week.

23. This famous Chancellor, who preserved his Humour and his Wit to the last Moment, when he came to be executed on _Tower-Hill_, the Headsman demanded his _upper Garment_ as his Fee; ay, Friend, said he, taking

off his _Cap_, That I think is my _Upper-Garment_.

24. The Great _Algernoon Sidney_ seemed to shew as little Concern at his Death, he had indeed got some Friends to intercede with the King for a Pardon; but when he was told, that his Majesty could not be prevailed upon to give him his Life, but that in Regard to his ancient and noble Family, he would remit Part of his Sentence, and only have his Head cut off; nay, said he, if his Majesty is resolved to have my _Head_ he may make a Whistle of my _A----_ if he pleases.

25. Lady _C----g_ and her two Daughters having taken Lodgings at a Leather-Breeches Maker's in _Piccadilly_, the Sign of the _Cock_ and _Leather-Breeches_, was always put to the Blush when she was obliged to give any Body Direction to her Lodgings, the Sign being so odd a one; upon which my Lady, a very good Sort of Woman, sending for her Landlord, a jolly young Fellow, told him, she liked him and his Lodgings very well, but she must be obliged to quit them on Account of his Sign, for she was ashamed to tell any body what it was, O! dear Madam, said the young Fellow, I would do any Thing rather than lose so good Lodgers, I can easily alter my Sign; so I think, answered my Lady, and I'll tell you how you may satisfy both me and my Daughters: _Only

take down your _Breeches_ and let your _Cock stand_.

26. When _Rablais_ the greatest Drole in _France_, lay on his Death-Bed, he could not help jesting at the very last Moment, for having received the extreme Unction, a Friend coming to see him, said, he hoped he was _prepared_ for the next World; Yes, yes, reply'd _Rablais_, I am ready for my Journey now, _they have just greased my Boots_.

27. _Henry_ the IVth, of _France_, reading an ostentatious Inscription on the Monument of a _Spanish_ Officer, _Here lies the Body of_ Don, &c., &c. _who never knew what Fear was_. _Then_ said the King, _he never snuffed a Candle with his Fingers_.

28. A certain Member of the _French_ Academy, who was no great Friend to the Abbot _Furetiere_, one Day took the Seat that was commonly used by the Abbot, and soon after having Occasion to speak, and _Furetiere_ being by that Time come in; Here is a Place, said he, Gentlemen, from when I am likely to utter a thousand Impertinences: Go on, answered _Furetiere_, there's _one_ already.

29. When Sir _Richard Steele_ was fitting up his great Room, in

York-Buildings, for publick Orations, that very Room, which is now so worthily occupied by the learned and eximious Mr. Professor _Lacy_. He happened at one Time to be pretty much behind Hand with his Workmen, and coming one Day among them to see how they went forward, he ordered one of them to get into the _Rostrum_, and make a Speech, that he might observe how it could be heard, the Fellow mounting, and scratching his Pate, told him he knew not what to say, for in Truth he was no Orator. Oh! said the Knight, no Matter for that, speak any thing that comes uppermost. Why here, Sir _Richard_, said the Fellow, we have been working for you these six Weeks, and cannot get one Penny of Money, pray, Sir, when do you design to pay us? Very well, very well, said Sir _Richard_, pray come down, I have heard enough, I cannot but own you speak very distinctly, tho' I don't admire your Subject.

30. A Country Clergyman meeting a Neighbour who never came to Church, altho' an old Fellow of above Sixty, he gave him some Reproof on that Account, and asked him if he never read at Home: No, replyed the Clown, I can't read; I dare say, said the Parson you don't know who made you; not I, in troth, said the Countryman. A little Boy coming by at the same Time, who made you, Child, cry'd the Parson, _God_, Sir, answered

the Boy. Why look you there, quoth the honest Clergyman, are not you ashamed to hear a Child of five or six Years old tell me who made him, when you that are so old a Man can not: Ah, said the Countryman, it is no Wonder that he should remember, he was made but t'other Day, it is a great while, Master, sin I were made.

31. A certain reverend Drone in the Country was complaining to another, that it was a great Fatigue to preach twice a Day. Oh! said the other, I preach twice every _Sunday_, and _make nothing of it_.

32. One of the foresaid Gentlemen, as was his Custom, preaching most exceedingly dull to a Congregation not used to him, many of them slunk out of the Church one after another, before the Sermon was near ended. Truly, said a Gentleman present, this learned Doctor has made a very _moving_ Discourse.

33. Sir _William Davenant_, the Poet, had _no Nose_, who going along the Meuse one Day, a Beggar-Woman followed him, crying, ah! God preserve your _Eye-Sight_; Sir, the Lord preserve your _Eye-Sight_. Why, good Woman, said he, do you pray so much for my _Eye-Sight_? Ah! dear Sir, answered the Woman, if it should please God that you grow

dim-sighted, you have no Place to hang your _Spectacles_ on.

34. A Welchman bragging of his Family, said, his Father's Effigies was set up in _Westminster-Abbey_, being ask'd whereabouts, he said in the same Monument with Squire _Thyne_'s for he was his Coachman.

35. A Person was saying, not at all to the Purpose, that really _Sampson_, was a very strong Man; Ay, said another, but you are much stronger, for you make nothing of lugging him by the Head and Shoulders.

36. My Lord _Strangford_, who stammered very much, was telling a certain Bishop that sat at his Table, that _Balaam_'s Ass spoke because he was Pri----est---- Priest-rid, Sir, said a Valet-de-Chambre, who stood behind his Chair, my Lord would say. No, Friend, reply'd the Bishop, _Balaam_ could not speak himself, and so his _Ass_ spoke for him.

37. The same noble Lord ask'd a Clergy-man once, at the Bottom of his Table, why the _Goose_, if there was one, was always plac'd next the _Parson_. Really, said he, I can give no Reason for it; but your

Question is so odd, that I shall never see a _Goose_ for the future without thinking of your _Lordship_.

38. A Gentleman was asking another how that poor Devil _S----ge_ could live, now my Lord _T----l_ had turn'd him off. Upon his Wits said the other; _That is living upon a slender Stock indeed_, reply'd the First.

39. A Country Parson having divided his Text under two and twenty Heads, one of the Congregation went out of the Church in a great Hurry, and being met by a Friend, he ask'd him, whither he was going? _Home for my Night-Cap_, answered the first, _For I find we are to stay here all Night_.

40. A very modest young Gentleman, of the County of _Tiperary_, having attempted many Ways in vain, to acquire the Affections of a Lady of great Fortune, at last try'd what was to be done, by the Help of Musick, and therefore entertained her with a Serenade under her Window,
at Midnight, but she ordered her Servants to drive him thence by throwing _Stones_ at him; _Your Musick, my Friend_, said one of his Companions, is as powerful as that of _Orpheus_, for it draws the very

Stones about you.

41. A certain Senator, who is not, it may be, esteemed the wisest Man in the House, has a frequent Custom of shaking his Head when another speaks, which giving Offence to a particular Person, he complained of the Affront; but one who had been long acquainted with him, assured the House, it was only an ill Habit he had got, for though he would oftentimes shake his _Head_, there was _nothing_ in it.

42. A Gentleman having lent a Guinea, for two or three Days, to a Person whose Promises he had not much Faith in, was very much surpriz'd to find he very punctually kept his Word with him; the same Gentleman being sometime after desirous of borrowing the like Sum, No, said the other, you have _deceived_ me once, and I am resolved you shan't do it a second Time.

43. My Lord Chief Justice Holt had sent, by his Warrant, one of the _French Prophets_, a foolish Sect, that started up in his Time, to Prison; upon which Mr. _Lacy_, one of their Followers, came one Day to my Lord's House, and desired to speak with him, the Servants told him, he was not well, and saw no Company that Day, but tell him, said

Lacy, I must see him, for I come to him from the _Lord God_, which being told the Chief Justice, he order'd him to come in, and ask'd him his Business; I come, said he, from the _Lord_, who sent me to thee, and would have thee grant a _Noli Prosequi_ for _John Atkins_, whom thou hast cast into Prison: Thou art a false Prophet, answered my Lord, and a lying Knave, for if the Lord had sent thee it wou'd have been to the _Attorney-General_, he knows it is not in my Power to grant a _Noli-Prosequi_.

44. _Tom B--rn--t_ happening to be at Dinner at my Lord Mayor's, in the latter Part of the late Queen's Reign, after two or three Healths, the Ministry was toasted, but when it came to _Tom_'s turn to drink, he diverted it for some Time by telling a Story to the Person who sat next him; the chief Magistrate of the City not seeing his Toast go round, call'd out, Gentlemen, _where sticks the Ministry_? At nothing, by G--d, says _Tom_, and so drank off his Glass.

45. My Lord _Craven_, in King _James_ the First's Reign, was very desirous to see _Ben Johnson_, which being told to _Ben_, he went to my Lord's House, but being in a very tatter'd Condition, as Poets sometimes are, the Porter refus'd him Admittance, with some saucy

Language, which the other did not fail to return: My Lord happening to come out while they were wrangling, asked the Occasion of it: _Ben_, who stood in need of no-body to speak for him, said, he understood his Lordship desired to see him; you, Friend, said my Lord, who are you? _Ben Johnson_, reply'd the other: No, no, quoth my Lord, you cannot be _Ben Johnson_ who wrote the _Silent Woman_, you look as if you could not say Bo to a Goose: _Bo_, cry'd _Ben_, very well, said my Lord, who was better pleas'd at the Joke, than offended at the Affront, I am now convinced, by your Wit, you are _Ben Johnson_.

46. A certain Fop was boasting in Company that he had every _Sense_ in Perfection; no, by G--d, said one, who was by, there is one you are entirely without, and that is _Common Sense_.

47. An _Irish_ Lawyer of the _Temple_, having occasion to go to Dinner, left these Directions written, and put in the Key-Hole of his Chamber-Door,
I am gone to the Elephant _and_ Castle, _where you shall find me_; and if _you can't read this Note, carry it down to the Stationer's, and he will read it for you_.

48. Old _Dennis_ who had been the author of many Plays, going by a

Brandy-Shop, in St. _Paul's Church-Yard_; the Man who kept it, came out to him, and desired him to drink a Dram, for what Reason said he, because you are a _Dramatick_ Poet, answered the other; well, Sir, said the old Gentleman, you are an out-of-the-way Fellow, and I will drink a Dram with you; but when he had so done, he asked him to pay for it, S'death, Sir, said the Bard, did you not ask me to drink a Dram because I was a _Dramatick_ Poet; yes Sir, reply'd the Fellow, but I did not think you had been a _Dram o'Tick_ Poet.

49. _Daniel Purcel_, the famous Punster, and a Friend of his, having a Desire to drink a Glass of Wine together, upon the 30th of _January_, they went to the _Salutation Tavern_ upon _Holbourn-Hill_, and finding the Door shut, they knock'd at it, but it was not opened to 'em, only one of the Drawers look'd through a little Wicket, and asked what they would please to have, why open your Door, said _Daniel_, and draw us a Pint of Wine, the Drawer said, his Master would not allow of it that Day, it was a _Fast_; D--mn your Master, cry'd he, for a precise Coxcomb, is he not contented to _fast_ himself but he must make his Doors _fast_ too.

50. The same Gentleman calling for some Pipes in a Tavern, complained

they were too _short_; the Drawer said they had no other, and those were but _just come in_: Ay, said _Daniel_, I see you have not bought them _very long_.

51. The same Gentleman as he had the Character of a great Punster, was desired one Night in Company, by a Gentleman, to make a _Pun extempore_, upon what Subject, said _Daniel_, the _King_, answered the other, the _King_, Sir, said he, is no _Subject_.

52. _G----s E----l_ who, tho' he is very rich, is remarkable for his sordid Covetousness, told _Cibber_ one Night, in the _Green Room_, that he was going out of Town, and was sorry to part with him, for faith _he loved him_, Ah! said _Colley_, I wish I was a Shilling for your sake, why so, said the other, because then, cry'd the Laureat, I should be sure _you loved me_.

53. Lord _C----by_ coming out of the House of Lords one Day, called out, where's my _Fellow_! Not in _England_, by G--d, said a Gentleman, who stood by.

54. A Beggar asking Alms under the Name of a poor Scholar, a Gentleman

to whom he apply'd himself, ask'd him a Question in _Latin_, the Fellow, shaking his Head, said he did not understand him: Why, said the Gentleman, did you not say you were a _poor Scholar_? _Yes_, reply'd the other, _a poor one indeed, Sir, for I don't understand one Word of_ Latin.

55. Several Years ago when Mrs. _Rogers_ the Player, was young and handsome, Lord _North_, and _Grey_, remarkable for his homely Face, accosting her one Night behind the Scenes, ask'd her with a Sigh, what was a _Cure for Love_? Your _Lordship_, said she, the best I know in the World.

56. Colonel ----, who made the fine Fire-Works Works in St. _James's Square_, upon the Peace of _Reswick_, being in Company with some Ladies, was highly commending the Epitaph just then set up in the Abbey on Mr. _Purcel's_ Monument,

> He _is gone to that Place were only his own_ Harmony _can be exceeded_.

Lord, Colonel, said one of the Ladies, the same Epitaph might serve for you, by altering one Word only:

He is gone to that Place, where only his own Fire-Works _can be exceeded_.

57. Poor _Joe Miller_ happening one Day to be caught by some of his Friends in a familiar Posture with a Cook Wench, almost as ugly as _Kate Cl--ve_, was very much rallied by them for the Oddness of his Fancy. Why look ye, said he, Gentleman, altho' I am not a very young Fellow, I have a good Constitution, and am not, I thank Heaven, reduced yet to _Beauty_ or _Brandy_ to whet my Appetite.

58. Lady _N----_, who had but a very homely Face, but was extremely well shaped, and always near about the Legs and Feet, was tripping one Morning over the _Park_ in a Mask; and a Gentleman followed her for a long while making strong Love to her, he called her his _Life_, his _Soul_, his _Angel_, and begged with abundance of Earnestness, to have a Glimpse of her Face; at last when she came on the other Side of the Bird-Cage Walk, to the House she was going into, she turned about and pulling off her Mask: Well, Sir, said she, what is it you would have with me? The Man at first Sight of her Face, drew back, and lifting up

his Hands, O! _Nothing!_ Madam, _Nothing_, cry'd he; I cannot say, said my Lady, but I like your Sincerity, tho' I hate your Manners.

60. Sir _B--ch--r W----y_, in the Beginning of Queen _Anne_'s Reign, and three or four more drunken Tories, reeling home from the _Fountain-Tavern_ in the _Strand_, on a _Sunday_ Morning, cry'd out, we are the pillars of the Church, no, by G--d, said a Whig, that happened to be in their Company, you can be but the _Buttresses_, for you never come on the Inside of it.

61. After the Fire of _London_, there was an Act of Parliament to regulate the Buildings of the City, every House was to be _three Stories_ high, and there were to be no _Balconies_ backwards: A _Gloucestershire_ Gentleman, a Man of great Wit and Humour, just after this Act passed, going along the Street, and seeing a little crooked Gentlewoman, on the other Side of the Way, he runs over to her in great haste, Lord, Madam, said he, how dare you to walk the Streets thus publickly? Walk the Streets! why not! answered the little Woman. Because said he, you are built directly contrary to Act of Parliament, you are but two Stories high, and your _Balcony_ hangs over your House-of-Office.

62. One Mr. _Topham_ was so very tall, that if he was living now, he might be shewn at _Yeate's_ Theatre for a Sight, this Gentleman going one Day to enquire for a Countryman a little Way out of Town, when he came to the House, he looked in at a little Window over the Door, and ask'd the Woman, who sat by the Fire, if her Husband was at Home. No, Sir, said she, but if you please to _alight_ and come in, I'll go and call him.

63. The same Gentleman walking across _Covent-Garden_, was asked by a Beggar-Woman, for an Half-penny or Farthing, but finding he would not part with his Money, she begg'd for Christ's-Sake, he would give her one of his old _Shoes_; he was very desirous to know what she could do with one Shoe, to make my Child a _Cradle_, Sir, said she.

64. King _Charles_ II. having ordered a Suit of Cloaths to be made, just at the Time when Addresses were coming up to him, from all Parts of the Kingdom, _Tom Killigrew_ went to the Taylor, and ordered him to make a very large Pocket on one Side of the Coat, and one so small on the other, that the King could hardly get his Hand into it, which seeming very odd, when they were brought home, he ask'd the Meaning of

it, the Taylor said, Mr. _Killigrew_ order'd it so; _Kelligrew_ being sent for, and interrogated, said, one Pocket was for the _Addresses_ of his Majesty's Subjects, the other for the _Money_ they would give him.

65. My Lord _B----e_, had married three Wives that were all his Servants, a Beggar-Woman, meeting him one Day in the Street, made him a very low Curtesy, Ah, God Almighty bless your Lordship, said she, and send you a long Life, if you do but live long enough, we shall be all _Ladies_ in Time.

66. Dr. _Tadloe_, who was a very fat Man, happening to go thump, thump, with his great Legs, thro' a Street, in _Oxford_, where some Paviers had been at Work, in the Midst of _July_, the Fellows immediately laid down their Rammers, Ah! God bless you, Master, cries one of 'em, it was very kind of you to come this Way, it saves us a great deal of Trouble this hot Weather.

67. An Arch-Wagg of St. _John_'s College, asked another of the same College, who was a great _Sloven_, why he would not read a certain Author called _Go-Clenius_.

68. _Swan_, the famous Punster of _Cambridge_, being a Nonjuror, upon which Account he had lost his Fellowship, as he was going along the _Strand_, in the Beginning of King _William_'s Reign, on a very rainy Day, a Hackney-Coachman called to him, Sir, won't you please to take Coach, it _rains_ hard: Ay, Friend, said he, but this is no _Reign_ for me to take Coach in.

69. When _Oliver_ first coined his Money, an old Cavalier looking upon one of the new Pieces, read the Inscriptions, on one Side was _God with us_, on the other, _The Commonwealth of_ England; I see, said he, God and the _Commonwealth_ are on _different_ Sides.

70. Colonel _Bond_ who had been one of King _Charles_ the First's Judges, dy'd a Day or two before _Oliver_, and it was strongly reported every where that _Cromwell_ was dead; No, said a Gentleman, who knew better, he has only given _Bond_ to the Devil for his farther Appearance.

71. Mr. Serjeant _G--d--r_, being _lame_ of one Leg; and pleading before Judge _For--e_, who has little or no _Nose_, the Judge told him he was afraid he had but a _lame_ Cause of it: Oh! my Lord, said the

Serjeant, have but a little Patience, and I'll warrant I prove every Thing as plain as the _Nose_ on your Face.

72. A Gentleman eating some Mutton that was very tough, said, it put him in Mind of an old _English_ Poet: Being asked who that was; _Chau--cer_, replied he.

73. A certain _Roman-Catholick_ Lord, having renounced the _Popish_ Religion, was asked not long after, by a Protestant Peer, _Whether the Ministers of the_ State, or _Ministers of the_ Gospel _had the greatest Share in his Conversion_: To whom he reply'd, that when he renounced _Popery_ he had also renounced auricular _Confession_.

74. _Michael Angelo_, in his Picture of the last Judgment, in the Pope's Chappel, painted among the Figures in _Hell_, that of a certain _Cardinal_, who was his Enemy, so like, that everybody knew it at first Sight: Whereupon the Cardinal complaining to Pope _Clement_ the Seventh, of the Affront, and desiring it might be defaced: You know very well, said the Pope, I have Power to deliver a Soul out of _Purgatory_ but not out of _Hell_.

75. A Gentleman being at Dinner at a Friend's House, the first Thing that came upon the Table was a Dish of Whitings, and one being put upon his Plate, he found it stink so much that he could not eat a Bit of it, but he laid his Mouth down to the Fish, as if he was whispering with it, and then took up the Plate and put it to his own Ear; the Gentleman, at whose Table he was, enquiring into the meaning, he told him he had a Brother lost at Sea, about a _Fortnight ago_, and he was asking that Fish if he knew any thing of him; and what Answer made he, said the Gentleman, he told me, said he, he could give no Account of him, for he had not been at Sea these _three Weeks_.

I would not have any of my Readers apply this Story, as an unfortunate Gentleman did, who had heard it, and was the next Day whispering a Rump

of Beef at a Friend's House.

76. An _English_ Gentleman happening to be in _Brecknockshire_, he used

sometimes to divert himself with shooting, but being suspected not to be qualified by one of the little _Welch_ Justices, his Worship told him, that unless he could produce his Qualification, he should not allow him to shoot there, and he had _two little Manors_; yes, Sir, said the _Englishman_, every Body may perceive that, perceive what, cry'd the _Welchman?_ That you have _too little Manners_, said the other.

77. The Chaplain's Boy of a Man of War, being sent out of his own Ship of an Errand to another; the two Boys were conferring Notes about their Manner of living; how often, said one, do you go to _Prayers_ now, why, answered the other, in Case of a _Storm_, or any Danger; ay, said the first, there's some Sense in that, but my Master makes us _pray_ when there is no more Occasion for it, than for my leaping over-board.

78. Not much unlike this Story, is one a Midshipman told one Night, in Company with _Joe Miller_ and myself, who said, that being once in great Danger at Sea, every body was observed to be upon their Knees, but one Man, who being called upon to come with the rest of the Hands to _Prayers_, not I, said he, it is your Business to take Care of the Ship I am but a _Passenger_.

79. Three or four roguish Scholars walking out one Day from the University of _Oxford_, spied a poor Fellow near _Abingdon_, asleep in a Ditch, with an Ass by him, loaded with Earthen-Ware, holding the

Bridle in his Hand, says one of the Scholars to the rest, if you'll assist me, I'll help you to a little Money, for you know we are bare at present; no doubt of it they were not long consenting; why then, said he, we'll go and sell this old Fellow's Ass at _Abingdon_, for you know the Fair is To-morrow, and we shall meet with Chapmen enough; therefore do you take the Panniers off, and put them upon my Back, and the Bridle over my Head, and then lead you the Ass to Market, and let me alone with the Old Man. This being done accordingly, in a little Time after the poor Man awaking, was strangely surprized to see his Ass thus metamorphosed; Oh! for God's-sake, said the Scholar, take this Bridle out of my Mouth, and this Load from my Back. Zoons, how came you here, reply'd the old Man, why, said he, my Father, who is a great Necromancer, upon an idle Thing I did to disoblige him, transformed me into an Ass, but now his Heart has relented, and I am come to my own Shape again, I beg you will let me go Home and thank him; by all Means, said the Crockrey Merchant, I don't desire to have any Thing to do with Conjuration, and so set the Scholar at Liberty, who went directly to his Comrades, that by this Time were making merry with the Money they had sold the Ass for: But the old Fellow was forced to go the next Day, to seek for a new one in the _Fair_, and after having look'd on several, his own was shewn him for a very good one, O, Ho! said he, _what have he and his Father quarrelled again already_? No, no, I'll have nothing to say to him.

80. Mr. _Congreve_ going up the Water, in a Boat, one of the Watermen told him, as they passed by _Peterborough_ House, that that House had _sunk a Story_; no, Friend, said he, I rather believe it is a _Story raised_.

81. The foresaid House, which is the very last in _London_ one Way, being rebuilt, a Gentleman asked another, who lived in it? his Friend told him Sir _Robert Grosvenor_; I don't know, said the first, what Estate Sir _Robert_ has, but he ought to have a very good one, for no body _lives beyond him in the whole Town_.

82. Two Gentlemen disputing about Religion, in _Button's Coffee-House_, said one of them, I wonder, Sir, you should talk of Religion, when I'll hold you five Guineas you can't say the _Lord's Prayer_, done, said the other, and Sir _Richard Steele_ shall hold Stakes. The Money being deposited, the Gentleman began with, _I believe in God_, and so went cleverly thro' the _Creed_; well, said the other, I own I have lost; _I

did not think he could have done it_.

83. A certain Author was telling Dr. _Sewel_, that a Passage he found fault with in his Poem, might be justify'd, and that he thought it a _Metaphor_; it is such a one, said the Doctor, as truly I never _Met-a-fore_.

84. A certain Lady at _Whitehall_, of great Quality but very little Modesty, having sent for a Linnen Draper to bring her some _Hollands_, as soon as the young Fellow enter'd the Room, O! Sir, said she, I find you're a Man fit for Business, for you no sooner look a Lady in the Face, but you've your _Yard_ in one Hand, and are lifting up the Linnen with the other.

85. A Country Farmer going cross his Grounds in the Dusk of the Evening, spy'd a young Fellow and a Lass, very busy near a five Bar Gate, in one of his Fields, and calling to them to know what they were about, said the young Man, no Harm, Farmer, we are only going to _Prop-a-Gate_.

86. King _Henry_ VIII. designing to send a _Nobleman_ on an Embassy

to _Francis_ I. at a very dangerous Juncture, he begg'd to be excused, saying such a threatening Message, to so hot a Prince as _Francis_ I. might go near to cost him his Life. Fear not, said old _Harry_, if the _French_ King should offer to take away your Life, I would revenge you by taking off the _Heads_ of many _Frenchmen_ now in my Power: _But of all those Heads_, reply'd the Nobleman, _there may not be one to fit my Shoulders_.

87. A Parson preaching a tiresome Sermon on _Happiness_ or _Bliss_; when he had done, a Gentleman told him, he had forgot one Sort of Happiness: _Happy are they that did not hear your Sermon_.

88. A Country-Fellow who was just come to _London_, gaping about in every Shop he came to, at last looked into a Scrivener's, where seeing only one Man sitting at a Desk, he could not imagine what Commodity was sold there, but calling to the Clerk, pray, Sir, said he, what do you sell here? _Loggerheads_, cry'd the other, _do you_, answer'd the Countryman, _Egad then you've a special Trade, for I see you have but one left_.

89. _Manners_, who was himself but lately made Earl of _Rutland_, told Sir _Thomas Moor_, he was too much elated by his Preferment, that he verify'd the old Proverb,

Honores mutant Mores.

No, my Lord, said Sir _Thomas_, the _Pun_ will do much better in _English_:

Honours change MANNERS.

90. A Nobleman having chose a very illiterate Person for his Library Keeper, one said it was like _a Seraglio kept by an Eunuch_.

91. A Mayor of _Yarmouth_, in ancient Times, being by his Office a Justice of the Peace, and one who was willing to dispense the Laws wisely, tho' he could hardly read, got him the Statute-Book, where finding a Law against _firing a Beacon_, or causing any _Beacon_ to be fired, after nine of the Clock at Night, the poor Man read it _frying of Bacon, or causing any Bacon to be fryed_; and accordingly went out the next Night upon the _Scent_, and being directed by his _Nose_, to

the Carrier's House, he found the Man and his Wife both _frying of Bacon_, the Husband holding the Pan while the Wife turned it: Being thus caught in the Fact, and having nothing to say for themselves, his Worship committed them both to Jail, without Bail or Mainprize.

92. The late facetious Mr. _Spiller_, being at the Rehearsal, on a _Saturday_ Morning, the Time when the Actors are usually paid, was asking another, whether Mr. _Wood_, the Treasurer of the House, had any Thing to say to them that Morning; no, faith, _Jemmy_, reply'd the other, I'm afraid there's no Cole, which is a cant Word for Money; by G--d, said _Spiller_, if there is no _Cole_ we must burn _Wood_.

93. A witty Knave coming into a Lace-Shop upon _Ludgate-Hill_, said, he had Occasion for a small Quantity of very fine Lace, and having pitched upon that he liked, asked the Woman of the Shop, how much she would have, for as much as would reach from one of his Ears to the other, and measure which Way she pleased, either over his Head or under his Chin; after some Words, they agreed, and he paid the Money down, and began to measure, saying, _One of my Ears is here, and the other is nailed to the Pillory in_ Bristol, _therefore, I fear you have not

enough to make good your Bargain; however, I will take this Piece in part, and desire you will provide the rest with all Expedition_.

94. When Sir _Cloudsly Shovel_ set out on his last Expedition, there was a Form of Prayer, composed by the Archbishop of _Canterbury_, for the Success of the Fleet, in which his Grace made Use of this unlucky Expression, that he begged God would be a _Rock_ of Defence to the Fleet, which occasioned the following Lines to be made upon the Monument, set up for him, in _Westminster-Abbey_, he being cast away in that Expedition, on the Rocks call'd, the _Bishop and his Clerks_.

  _As_ Lambeth _pray'd_, such was the dire Event,
  Else had we wanted now this Monument;
  That God unto our Fleet would be a Rock,
  Nor did kind Heav'n, the wise Petition mock;
  To what the_ Metropolitan _said then,
  The_ Bishop and his Clerks _reply'd_, Amen.

95. A _French_ Marquis being once at Dinner at _Roger Williams's_, the famous Punster and Publican, and boasting of the happy Genius of his Nation, in projecting all the fine Modes and Fashions, particularly

the _Ruffle_, which he said, _was de fine Ornament to de Hand, and had been followed by all de oder Nations_: _Roger_, allowed what he said, but observed, at the same Time, that the English, according to Custom, had made a great Improvement upon their Invention, _by adding the Shirt to it_.

96. A poor dirty Shoe-Boy going into a Church, one _Sunday_ Evening, and seeing the Parish-Boys standing in a Row, upon a Bench to be catechized, he gets up himself, and stands in the very first Place, so the Parson of Course beginning with him, asked him, _What is your Name_? _Rugged_ and _Tough_, answered he, _who gave you that Name_?
says Domine: _Why the Boys in our Alley_, reply'd poor _Rugged_ and _Tough, Lord d--mn them_.

97. A Prince laughing at one of his Courtiers whom he had employed in several Embassies, told him, he looked like an _Owl_. I know not, answered the Courtier, what I look like; but this I know, that I have had the Honour several Times to represent your _Majesty's Person_.

98. A _Venetian_ Ambassador going to the Court of _Rome_, passed through _Florence_, where he went to pay his Respects to the late

Duke of _Tuscany_. The Duke complaining to him of the Ambassador the State of _Venice_ had sent him, as a Man unworthy of his Publick Character; _Your Highness_, said he, _must not wonder at it, for we have many Idle Pates, at_ Venice. _So have we_, reply'd the Duke, in Florence; _but we don't send them to treat of Publick Affairs_.

99. A Lady's Age happening to be questioned, she affirmed, she was but _Forty_, and call'd upon a Gentleman that was in Company for his Opinion; Cousin, said she, do you believe I am in the Right, when I say I am but _Forty_? I ought not to dispute it, Madam, reply'd he, for I have heard you say so _these ten Years_.

100. It being proved in a Trial at _Guild-Hall_, that a Man's Name was really _Inch_, who pretended that it was _Linch_, I see, said the Judge, the old Proverb is verified in this Man, who being allowed an _Inch_ took an _L_.

101. A certain Person came to a Cardinal in _Rome_, and told him that he had brought his Eminence a dainty white _Palfrey_, but he fell lame by the Way; saith the Cardinal to him, I'll tell thee what thou shalt do, go to such a Cardinal, and such a one, naming half a Dozen, and

tell them the same, and so as thy Horse, if it had been _sound_, could have pleas'd but _one_, with this _lame Horse_ thou shalt please half a Dozen.

102. A prodigal Gallant (whose penurious Mother being lately dead, had left him a plentiful Estate) one Day being on his Frolicks, quarrell'd with his Coachman, and said, you damn'd Son of a Whore, I'll kick you into Hell; to which the Coachman answer'd, _if you kick me into Hell, I'll tell your Mother how extravagantly you spend your Estate here upon Earth_.

103. The Emperor _Augustus_, being shewn a young _Grecian_, who very much resembled him, asked the young Man if his _Mother_ had not been at
Rome: No, Sir, answer'd the _Grecian_ but my _Father_ has.

104. _Cato_ the Censor being ask'd, how it came to pass, that he had no Statue erected for him, who had so well deserved of the Common-Wealth?
I had rather, said he, have this Question asked, than _why I had one_.

105. A Lady coming into a Room hastily, with her _Mantua_, brush'd down a _Cremona_ Fiddle, that lay on a Chair, and broke it, upon which a Gentleman that was present burst into this Exclamation from _Virgil_:

Mantua væ miseræ nimium Vicina Cremona.

Ah miserable Mantua _too near a Neighbour to_ Cremona.

106. A devout Gentleman, being very earnest in his Prayers, in the Church, it happened that a Pick-Pocket being near him, stole away his _Watch_, who having ended his Prayers, mist it, and complained to his Friend, that his _Watch_ was lost, while he was at Prayers; to which his friend reply'd, _Had you watch'd as well as pray'd, your Watch had been secure, adding these following Lines_.

_He that a Watch will wear, this must he do,
Pocket his Watch, and watch his Pocket too._

107. _George Ch----n_, who was always accounted a very blunt Speaker, asking a young Lady one Day, what it was o'Clock, and she telling him her Watch _stood_, I don't wonder at that, Madam, said he, when it is

so near your ----.

108. A modest Gentlewoman being compelled by her Mother to accuse her Husband of Defect, and being in the Court, she humbly desired of the Judge, that she might write her Mind, and not be obliged to speak it, for Modesty's sake; the Judge gave her that Liberty, and a Clerk was immediately commanded to give her Pen, Ink, and Paper, whereupon she took the Pen without dipping it into the Ink, and made as if she would write; says the Clerk to her, Madam, there is no Ink in your Pen. _Truly, Sir_, says she, _that's just my Case, and therefore I need not explain myself any further_.

109. A Lieutenant Colonel to one of the _Irish_ Regiments, in the _French_ Service, being dispatched by the Duke of _Berwick_, from _Fort Kehl_, to the King of _France_, with a Complaint, relating to some Irregularities, that had happened in the Regiment; his _Majesty_, with some Emotion of Mind, told him, _That the_ Irish _Troops gave him more Uneasiness than all his Forces besides_. _Sir_, (says the Officer) _all your Majesty's Enemies make the same Complaint_.

110. Mr. _G----n_, the Surgeon being sent for to a Gentleman, who had

just received a slight Wound in a Rencounter, gave Orders to his Servant to go Home with all haste imaginable, and fetch a certain Plaister; the Patient turning a little Pale, Lord, Sir, said he, _I hope there is no Danger_. _Yes, indeed is there_, answered the Surgeon, _for if the Fellow don't set up a good pair of Heels, the Wound will heal before he returns_.

111. Not many Years ago, a certain Temporal Peer, having in a most pathetick and elaborate Speech, exposed the Vices and Irregularities of the Clergy, and vindicated the Gentlemen of the Army from some Imputations unjustly laid upon them: A Prelate, irritated at the Nature, as well as the Length of the Speech, _desired to know when the Noble Lord would leave off preaching_. The other answer'd, _The very Day he was made a Bishop_.

112. It chanc'd that a Merchant Ship was so violently tossed in a Storm at Sea that all despairing of Safety, betook themselves to Prayer, saving one Mariner, who was ever wishing to see two _Stars_: Oh! said he, that I could but see two Stars, or but one of the Two, and of these Words he made so frequent Repetition, that, disturbing the Meditations of the rest, at length one asked him, what two Stars, or what one Star

he meant? To whom he reply'd, _O! that I could but see the Star in Cheapside, or the Star in_ Coleman-street, _I care not which_.

113. A Country Fellow subpoeena'd for a Witness upon a Trial on an Action of Defamation, he being sworn, the Judge had him repeat the very same Words he had heard spoken; the Fellow was loath to speak, but humm'd and haw'd for a good Space, but being urged by the Judge, he at last spoke, _My Lord_, said he, _You are a Cuckold_: The Judge seeing the People begin to laugh, called to him, and had him speak to the _Jury, there were twelve of them_.

114. A Courtier, who was a Confident of the Amours of _Henry_ IV. of _France_, obtained a Grant from the King, for the Dispatch whereof he applyed himself to the Lord High Chancellor: Who finding some Obstacle in it, the Courtier still insisted upon it, and would not allow of any Impediment, _Que chacun se mêle de son Metier_, said the Chancellor to him; that is, _Let every one meddle with his own Business_. The Courtier imagining he reflected upon him for his pimping; _my Employment_, said he, _is such, that, if the King were twenty Years younger I would not exchange it for three of your's_.

115. A Gentlewoman, who thought her Servants always cheated her, when they went to _Billingsgate_ to buy Fish, was resolved to go thither one Day herself, and asking the Price of some Fish, which she thought too dear, she bid the Fish-Wife about half what she asked; Lord, Madam, said the Woman, I must have stole it to sell it at that Price, but you shall have it if you will tell me what you do to make your Hands look so white; Nothing, good Woman, answered the Gentlewoman, but wear _Dog-Skin Gloves_: D--mn you for a lying Bitch, reply'd the other, my Husband has wore _Dog-Skin Breeches_ these ten Years, and his A--se is as brown as a Nutmeg.

116. Dr. _Heylin_, a noted Author, especially for his _Cosmography_, happened to lose his Way going to _Oxford_, in the Forest of _Whichwood_: Being then attended by one of his Brother's Men, the Man earnestly intreated him to lead the Way; but the Doctor telling him he did not know it: _How!_ said the Fellow, _that's very strange that you, who have made a Book of the whole World, cannot find the Way out of this little Wood_.

117. Monsieur _Vaugelas_ having obtained a Pension from the _French_ King, by the Interest of Cardinal _Richelieu_, the Cardinal told him,

he hoped he would not forget the Word _Pension_ in his Dictionary. No, my Lord, said _Vaugelas_, nor the Word _Gratitude_.

118. A melting Sermon being preached in a Country Church, all fell a weeping but one Man, who being asked, why he did not weep with the rest? O! said he, _I belong to another Parish_.

119. A Gentlewoman growing big with Child, who had two Gallants, one of them with a wooden Leg, the Question was put, which of the two should father the Child. He who had the wooden Leg offer'd to decide it thus. _If the Child_, said he, _comes into the World with a wooden Leg, I will father it, if not, it must be your's_.

120. A Gentleman who had been out a shooting brought home a small Bird with him, and having an _Irish_ Servant, he ask'd him, if he had shot that little Bird, yes, he told him; Arrah! by my Shoul, Honey, reply'd the _Irish_ Man, it was not worth Powder and Shot, for this little Thing would have _died in the Fall_.

121. The same _Irishman_ being at a Tavern where the Cook was dressing

some Carp, he observed that some of the Fish moved after they were gutted and put in the Pan, which very much surprizing Teague, well, now, faith, said he, _of all the Christian Creatures that ever I saw, this same Carp will live the longest after it is dead_.

122. A Gentleman happening to turn up against an House to make Water, did not see two young Ladies looking out of a Window close by him, 'till he heard them giggling, then looking towards them, he asked, what made them so merry? O! Lord, Sir, said one of them, _a very little Thing_ will make us laugh.

123. A Gentleman hearing a Parson preach upon the Story of the Children being devoured by the two _She Bears_, who reviled the old Man, and not much liking his Sermon; some Time after seeing the same Parson come into the Pulpit to preach at another Church: O ho! said he, _What are you here with your_ Bears _again_.

124. A young Fellow riding down a steep Hill, and doubting that the Foot of it was boggish, call'd out to a Clown that was ditching, and ask'd him, if it was hard at the Bottom: Ay, ay, answered the Countryman, it's hard enough at the Bottom I'll warrant you: But in

half a Dozen Steps the Horse sunk up to the Saddle Skirts, which made the young Gallant whip, spur, curse and swear, why thou Whoreson Rascal, said he, to the Ditcher, did'st thou not tell me it was hard at Bottom? _Ay_, reply'd the other, _but you are not half Way to the Bottom yet_.

125. It was said of one who remembered every Thing that he lent, but quite forgot what he borrowed, _That he had lost half his Memory_.

126. One speaking of _Titus Oats_, said, he was a Villain in Grain, and deserved to be well _threshed_.

127. It was said of _Henry_, Duke of _Guise_, that he was the greatest Usurer in all _France_, for he had turned all his Estate into _Obligations_, meaning, he had sold and mortgaged his Patrimony, to make Presents to other Men.

128. An _Englishman_ and a _Welchman_ disputing in whose Country was the best Living, said the _Welchman_, there is such noble Housekeeping in _Wales_, that I have known above a Dozen Cooks employ'd at one Wedding Dinner; Ay, answered the _Englishman_, that was because every

Man _toasted his own Cheese_.

129. The late Sir _Godfrey Kneller_, had always a very great Contempt, I will not pretend to say how justly, for _J----s_ the Painter, and being one Day about twenty Miles from _London_, one of his Servants told him at Dinner, that there was Mr. _J----s_ come that Day into the same Town with a Coach and four: Ay, said Sir _Godfrey_, but if his Horses _draw_ no better than himself, they'll never carry him to Town again.

130. Some Women speaking of the Pains of Childbirth, for my Part, said one of them, it is less Trouble to me, than to swallow a Poach'd Egg: Then sure, Madam, answer'd another, your _Throat_ is very narrow.

131. A Gentleman asked _Nanny Rochford_, why the Whigs, in their Mourning for Queen _Anne_, all wore Silk Stockings: Because, said she, the Tories _were worsted_.

132. A Counsellor pleading at the Bar with Spectacles on, who was blind with one Eye, said, he would produce nothing but what was _ad Rem_, then said one of the adverse Party, _You must take out one Glass of

your Spectacles, which I am sure is of no Use_.

133. The famous _Tom Thynn_, who was remarkable for his good Housekeeping and Hospitality, standing one Day at his Gate in the Country, a Beggar coming up to him, cry'd, he begg'd his Worship would give him a Mugg of his _Small Beer_: Why how now, said he, what Times are these! _when Beggars must be Choosers_. I say, bring this Fellow a Mugg of _Strong Beer_.

134. It was said of a Person, who always eat at _other Peoples Tables_, and was a great _Railer_, that he never opened _his Mouth_ but to some Body's Cost.

135. Pope _Sixtus Quintus_, who was a poor Man's Son, and his Father's House ill thatched, so that the Sun came in at many Places of it, would himself make a Jest of his Birth, and say, _that he was_, Nato di Casa illustre, _Son of an illustrious House_.

136. _Diogenes_ begging, as was the Custom among many Philosophers, asked a _prodigal Man_ for more than any one else: Whereupon one said to him, _I see your Business, that when you find a liberal Mind, you

will take most of him_: _No_, said _Diogenes, but I mean to beg of the rest again_.

137. Dr. _Sewel_, and two or three Gentlemen, walking towards _Hampstead_ on a Summer's Day, were met by the famous _Daniel Purcel_, who was very importunate with them to know upon what Account they were going there; the Doctor merrily answering him, _to make Hay_; Very well, reply'd the other, you'll be there at a very convenient Season, the Country wants _Rakes_.

138. A Gentleman speaking of his Servant, said, _I believe I command more than any Man, for before my Servant will obey me in one Thing, I must command him ten Times over_.

139. A poor Fellow that was carrying to Execution had a Reprieve just as he came to the Gallows, and was carried back by a Sheriff's Officer, who told him, he was a happy Fellow, and asked him, if he knew nothing of the Reprieve before-hand; no, reply'd the Fellow, nor thought any more of it, than I did of my _Dying Day_.

140. A _Spanish_ Lady reading, in a _French_ Romance, a long Conversation betwixt two Lovers; _What a deal of Wit_, said she, _is here thrown away, when two Lovers are got together, and no Body by_?

141. A Countryman admiring the stately Fabrick of St. _Paul's_, ask'd, _whether it was made in_ England, or _brought from beyond Sea_?

142. _Fabricus_ the _Roman_ Consul, shew'd a great Nobleness of Mind, when the Physician of King _Pyrrhus_ made him a Proposal to poison his Master, by sending the Physician back to _Pyrrhus_, with these Words; _Learn, O King! to make a better Choice of thy_ Friends _and of thy_ Foes.

143. A Lady, who had generally a pretty many Intrigues upon her Hands, not liking her Brother's extravagant Passion for Play, asked him, when he designed to leave off _Gaming_; when you cease _Loving_, said he; then reply'd the Lady, _you are like to continue a Gamester as long as you live_.

144. A Soldier was bragging before _Julius Cæsar_, of the Wounds he had received in his Face; _Cæsar_, knowing him to be a Coward, told him, he

had best take heed, the next Time he ran away, _how he look'd back_.

145. The _Trojans_ sending Ambassadors to condole with _Tiberius_ upon the Death of his Father-in-Law _Augustus_, it was so long after, that the Emperor hardly thought it a Compliment, but told them he was likewise sorry _that they had lost so valiant a Knight_ as Hector, who was slain above a thousand Years before.

146. _Cato Major_ used to say, _That wise Men learned more from_ Fools,
than Fools _from wise Men_.

147. A _Braggadochio_ chancing, upon an Occasion, to run away full Speed, was asked by one, what was become of that Courage he used so much to talk of, it is got, said he, _all into my Heels_.

148. Somebody asked my Lord _Bacon_ what he thought of _Poets_, why, said he, I think them the very best Writers next to those who write in Prose.

149. A Profligate young Nobleman, being in Company with some sober People, desired leave to toast the _Devil_; the Gentleman who sat next

him, said, he had no Objection to any of his Lordship's Friends.

150. A _Scotsman_ was very angry with an _English_ Gentleman, who, he said, had abused him, and called him _false Scot_; Indeed, said the _Englishman_, I said no such Thing, but that you were a _true Scot_.

151. The late Commissary-General _G--ley_, who once kept a Glass Shop, having General _P--c--k's_ Regiment under a Muster, made great Complaints of the Men's Appearance, &c. and said, _that the Regiment ought to be broke:_ Then, Sir_, said the Colonel, _perhaps you think a Regiment is as soon broke as a Looking-Glass_.

152. _C----ll_, the Bookseller, being under Examination, at the Bar of the House of Lords, for publishing the Posthumous Works of the late Duke of _Buckingham_, without Leave of the Family, told their Lordships in his Defence, _That if the Duke was_ living, _he was sure he would readily pardon the Offence_.

153. A Gentleman said of a young Wench, who constantly ply'd about the _Temple_, that if she had as much Law in her _Head_, as she had had in her _Tail_, she would be one of the ablest _Counsel_ in _England_.

154. _J--ck K----s_, the Painter, having finish'd a very good Picture of _Figg_ the Prize-Fighter, who had been famous for getting the better of several _Irishmen_ of the same Profession, the Piece was shewn to old _J----n_, the Player, who was told at the same Time, that Mr. _E----s_ designed to have a Mezzo-tinto Print taken from it, but wanted a Motto to be put under it: Then said old _J----n_, I'll give you one: _A Figg for the Irish_.

155. Some Gentlemen going into a noted Bawdy-House Tavern at _Charing-Cross_, found great Fault with the Wine, and sending for the Master of the House, told him, it was sad Stuff, and very _weak_: It may be so, said he, for my Trade don't depend upon the _Strength_ of my _Wine_, but on that of my Tables and Chairs.

156. A Gentleman coming to an Inn in _Smithfield_, and seeing the Hostler expert and tractable about the Horses, asked, _how long he had lived there_? And _What Countryman he was_? _I'se Yerkshire_, said the Fellow, _an ha'_ lived _Sixteen Years here_. I wonder reply'd the Gentleman, that in so long a Time, so clever a Fellow as you seem to be, have not come to be Master of the Inn yourself. Ay, said the

Hostler, _But Maister's Yerkshire_ too.

157. The late Colonel _Chartres_, reflecting on his ill Life and Character, told a certain Nobleman, that if such a Thing as a good Name was to be purchased, he would freely give 10,000 Pounds for one; the Nobleman said, _it would certainly be the worst Money he ever laid out in his Life_. Why so, said the honest Colonel, _because_, answered my Lord, _you would forfeit it again in less than a Week_.

158. A seedy [poor] half-pay Captain, who was much given to blabbling every thing he heard, was told, there was but one Secret in the World he could keep, and that was _where he lodged_.

159. _Jack M----n_, going one Day into the Apartments at St. _James's_, found a Lady of his Acquaintance sitting in one of the Windows, who very courteously asked him, to sit down by her, telling him there was a _Place, No, Madam_, said he, _I don't come to Court for a Place_.

If the gentle Reader should have a Desire to repeat this Story let him not make the same Blunder that a certain _English-Irish foolish_ Lord did, who made the Lady ask _Jack_ to sit down by her, telling him there was _room_.

160. A certain Lady of Quality sending her _Irish_ Footman to fetch Home a Pair of new Stays, strictly charged him to take a Coach if it rained for fear of wetting them: But a great Shower of Rain falling, the Fellow returned with the Stays dropping wet, and being severely reprimanded for not doing as he was ordered, he said, he had obey'd his Orders; how then, answered the Lady, could the Stays be wet, if you took them into the Coach with you? _No_, replyed honest Teague, _I knew
my Place better, I did not go into the Coach, but rode_ behind _as I always used to do_.

161. _Tom Warner_, the late Publisher of News Papers and Pamphlets, being very near his End, a Gentlewoman in the Neighbourhood sending her
Maid to enquire how he did, he had the girl tell her Mistress, _that he hoped he was going to the_ New-Jerusalem; _Ah, dear Sir_, said she, _I dare say the Air of_ Islington _would do you more good_.

162. A Person said the _Scotch_ were certainly the best trained up for Soldiers of any People in the World, for they began to _handle their

Arms_ almost as soon as they were born.

163. A Woman once prosecuted a Gentleman for a Rape: Upon the trial, the Judge asked if she made any Resistance, _I cry'd out, an please you my Lord_, said she: _Ay_, said one of the Witnesses, _but that was Nine Months after_.

164. A young Lady who had been married but a short Time, seeing her Husband going to rise pretty early in the Morning, said, _What, my Dear, are you getting up already? Pray, lie_ a little longer and rest yourself. _No, my Dear_, reply'd the Husband, _I'll get up and rest myself_.

165. The Deputies of _Rochel_, attending to speak with _Henry_ the Fourth of _France_, met with a Physician who had renounced the Protestant Religion, and embrac'd the Popish Communion, whom they began to revile most grievously. The King hearing of it, told the Deputies, he advis'd them to change their Religion, _for it is a dangerous Symptom_, says he, _that your religion is not long-liv'd, when a Physician has given it over_.

166. Two _Oxford_ Scholars meeting on the Road with a _Yorkshire_ Ostler, they fell to bantering the Fellow, and told him, they could prove him a Horse, an Ass, and I know not what; and I, said the Ostler, can prove your Saddle to be me a _Mule_: A _Mule!_ cried one of them, how can that be? because, said the Ostler, it is something between a _Horse_ and an _Ass_.

167. A _Frenchman_ travelling between _Dover_ and _London_, came into an Inn to lodge, where the Host perceiving him a close-fisted Cur, having called for nothing but a Pint of Beer and a Pennyworth of Bread to eat with a Sallad he had gathered by the Way, resolved to fit him for it, therefore seemingly paid him an extraordinary Respect, laid him a clean Cloth for Supper, and complimented him with the best Bed in the House. In the Morning he set a good Sallad before him, with Cold Meat, Butter, _&c_., which provok'd the Monsieur to the Generosity of calling for half a Pint of Wine; then coming to pay, the Host gave him a Bill, which, for the best Bed, Wine, Sallad, and other Appurtenances, he had enhanc'd to the Value of twenty Shillings. _Jernie_, says the _Frenchman_, Twenty Shillings! _Vat you mean?_ But all his sputtering was in vain; for the Host with a great deal of Tavern-Elocution, made him sensible that nothing could be 'bated. The Monsieur therefore

seeing no Remedy but Patience, seem'd to pay it chearfully. After which he told the Host, that his House being extremely troubled with Rats, he could give him a Receipt to drive 'em away, so as they should never return again. The Host being very desirous to be rid of those troublesome Guests, who were every Day doing him one Mischief or other, at length concluded to give Monsieur twenty Shillings for a Receipt; which done, _Beggar_, says the Monsieur, _you make a de Rat one such Bill as you make me, and if ever dey trouble your House again, me will be hang_.

168. A young Gentleman playing at Questions and Commands with some very pretty young Ladies, was commanded to take off a Garter from one of them; but she, as soon as he had laid hold of her Petticoats, ran away into the next Room, where was a Bed, now, Madam, said he, I _bar_ squeaking, _Bar_ the Door, you Fool, cry'd she.

169. A _Westminster_ Justice taking Coach in the City, and being set down at _Young Man's_ Coffee-house, _Charing-Cross_, the Driver demanded Eighteen-Pence as his Fare; the Justice asked him, if he would swear that the Ground came to the Money; the Man said, he would take

his Oath on't. The Justice replyed, _Friend, I am a Magistrate_, and pulling a Book out of his Pocket, administer'd the Oath, and then gave the Fellow _Six-pence_, saying _he must reserve the Shilling to himself for the_ Affidavit.

170. A Countryman passing along the _Strand_ saw a Coach overturn'd, and asking what the Matter was? He was told, that three or four Members of Parliament were overturned in that Coach: Oh, says he, there let them lie, _my Father always advis'd me not to meddle with State Affairs_.

171. One saying that Mr. _Dennis_ was an excellent Critick, was answered, that indeed his Writings were much to be valued; for that by his Criticism he taught Men how to write well, and by his Poetry, shew'd 'em what it was to write ill; so that the World was sure to edify by him.

172. One going to see a Friend who had lain a considerable Time in the _Marshalsea_ Prison, in a Starving Condition, was persuading him, rather than lie there in that miserable Case, to go to Sea; which not agreeing with his high Spirit, _I thank you for your Advice_, replies

the Prisoner, _but if I go to Sea, I'm resolv'd it shall be upon good Ground_.

173. A Drunken Fellow carrying his Wife's Bible to pawn for a Quartern of Gin, to an Alehouse, the Man of the House refused to take it. What a Pox, said the Fellow, will neither my Word, nor the Word of G--d pass?

174. A certain Justice of Peace, not far from _Clerkenwell_, in the first Year of King _George_ I. when his Clerk was reading a Mittimus to him, coming to _Anno Domini_ 1714, cry'd out, with some warmth, and _why not Georgeo Domini, sure, Sir, you forget yourself strangely_.

175. A certain Noblem--, a Cour--r, in the Beginning of the late Reign, coming out of the H--se of L--ds, accosts the Duke of _B--ham_, with, _How does your Pot boil, my Lord, these troublesome Times?_ To which his Grace replied, I never go into my Kitchen, but I dare say the _Scum is uppermost_.

176. A little dastardly half-witted 'Squire, being once surpriz'd by his Rival in his Mistress's Chamber, of whom he was terribly afraid, desir'd for God's Sake to be conceal'd; but there being no Closet or

Bed in the Room, nor indeed any Place proper to hold him, but an _India_ Chest the Lady put her Cloathes in, they lock'd him in there. His Man being in the same Danger with himself, said, rather than fail, he cou'd creep under the Maid's Petticoats: _Oh, you silly Dog_, says his Master, _that's the commonest Place in the House_.

177. The Lord _N----th_ and _G----y_, being once at an Assembly at the _Theatre-Royal_ in the _Hay-Market_, was pleas'd to tell Mr. _H--d--gg--r_, he wou'd make him a Present of 100_l._ if he could produce an uglier Face in the whole Kingdom than his, the said _H--d--gg--r_'s, within a Year and a Day: Mr. _H--d--gg--r_ went instantly and fetch'd a Looking-Glass, and presented it to his Lordship, saying, _He did not doubt but his Lordship had Honour enough to keep his Promise_.

178. A young Fellow praising his Mistress before a very amorous Acqaintance of his, after having run thro' most of her Charms, he came at Length to her Majestick Gate, fine Air, and delicate slender Waist: _Hold_, says his Friend, _go no lower, if you love me_; but by your Leave, says the other, _I hope to go lower if she loves me_.

179. A Person who had an unmeasurable Stomach, coming to a Cook's Shop to dine, said, it was not his Way to have his Meat cut, but to pay 8_d._ for his _Ordinary_; which the Cook seem'd to think reasonable enough, and so set a Shoulder of Mutton before him, of half a Crown Price, to cut where he pleas'd; with which he so play'd the Cormorant, that he devour'd all but the Bones, paid his _Ordinary_, and troop'd off. The next Time he came, the Cook casting a Sheep's Eye at him, desired him to agree for his Victuals, for he'd have no more _Ordinaries_. Why, a Pox on you, says he, _I'm sure I paid you an_ Ordinary _Price_.

180. The extravagant Duke of _Buckingham [Villars]_ once said in a melancholy Humour, he was afraid he should _die a Beggar_, which was the most terrible Thing in the World; upon which a Friend of his Grace's replyed, No, my Lord, there is a more terrible Thing than that, and which you have Reason to fear, and that is, _that you'll live a_ Beggar_.

181. The same Duke another Time was making his Complaint to Sir _John Cutler_, a rich Miser, of the Disorder of his Affairs, and asked him, what he should do to prevent the Ruin of his Estate? _Live as I do, my_

Lord_, said Sir _John: That I can do_, answered the Duke, _when I am_ ruined.

182. At another Time, a Person who had long been a Dependant on his Grace, begged his Interest for him at Court, and to press the Thing more home upon the Duke, said, _He had no Body to depend on but God and his Grace; then_, says the Duke, _you are in a miserable Way, for you could not have pitch'd upon any two Persons who have less Interest at Court_.

183. The old Lord _Strangford_ taking a Bottle with the Parson of the Parish, was commending his own Wine: _Here, Doctor_, says he, _I can send a couple of Ho--Ho--Ho--Hounds to_ France (for his Lordship had an Impediment in his Speech) _and have a Ho--Ho--Ho--Hogshead of this Wi--Wi--Wi--Wine for 'em; What do you say to that, Doctor? Why_, I say, _your Lordship has your Wine-Dog-cheap_.

184. The famous _Jack Ogle_ of facetious Memory, having borrow'd on Note five Pounds and failing the Payment, the Gentleman who had lent it, indiscreetly took Occasion to talk of it in the Publick Coffee-house which oblig'd _Jack_ to take Notice of it, so that it came

to a Challenge. Being got into the Field, the Gentleman a little tender in Point of Courage, offer'd him the Note to make the Matter up; to which our Hero consented readily, and had the Note delivered: _But now_, said the Gentleman, _If we should return without fighting, our Companions will laugh at us; therefore let's give one another a slight Scar, and say we wounded one another; with all my Heart_, says _Jack; Come, I'll wound you first_; so drawing his Sword, he whipt it thro' the fleshy Part of his Antagonist's Arm, 'till he brought the very Tears in his Eyes. This being done, and the Wound ty'd up with a Handkerchief; Come, says the Gentleman, _now where shall I wound you_?

Jack putting himself in a fighting Posture, cried, _Where you can, B----d Sir; Well, well_, says the other, _I can swear I received this Wound of you_, and so march'd off contentedly.

185. A Traveller at an Inn once on a very cold Night, stood so near the Fire that he burnt his Boots: An arch Rogue that sat in the Chimney-Corner, call'd out to him, _Sir, you'll burn your Spurs presently_: _My Boots you mean, I suppose_: _No Sir,_ says he, _they are burnt already_.

186. In Eighty-Eight, when Queen _Elizabeth_ went from _Temple-Bar_

along _Fleet-street_, on some Procession, the Lawyers were rang'd on one Side of the Way, and the Citizens on the other; says the Lord _Bacon_, then a Student, to a Lawyer, that stood next him, _Do but observe the Courtiers; if they bow first to the Citizens, they are in Debt; if to us, they are in Law_.

187. Some Gentlemen having a Hare for Supper at the Tavern, the Cook, instead of a Pudding, had cramm'd the Belly full of _Thyme_, but had not above half roasted the Hare, the Legs being almost raw; which one of the Company observing said, _There was too much Thyme, or Time, in the Belly, and too little in the Legs._

188. Two Countrymen who had never seen a Play in their Lives, nor had any Notion of it, went to the Theatre in _Drury-Lane_, when they placed themselves snug in the Corner of the Middle-Gallery; the first Musick play'd, which they lik'd well enough; then the Second, and the Third to their great Satisfaction: At Length the Curtain drew up, and three or four Actors enter'd to begin the Play; upon which one of them cry'd to the other, _Come_, Hodge, _let's be going, ma'haps the Gentlemen are talking about Business_.

189. A Countryman sowing his Ground, two smart Fellows riding that Way, call'd to him with an insolent Air: _Well, honest Fellow_, says one of them, _'tis your Business to sow, but we reap the Fruits of your Labour_; to which the plain Countryman reply'd, _'Tis very likely you may, truly, for I am sowing_ Hemp.

190. Two inseparable Comrades, who rode in the Guards in _Flanders_, had every Thing in common between them. One of them being a very extravagant Fellow, and unfit to be trusted with Money, the other was always Purse-bearer, which yet he gain'd little by, for the former would at Night frequently pick his Pocket to the last _Stiver_; to prevent which he bethought himself of a Stratagem, and coming among his Companions the next Day, he told them _he had bit his Comrade_. _Ay, how?_ says they. _Why_, says he, _I hid my Money in his own Pocket last Night, and I was sure he would never look for it there_.

191. The famous Sir _George Rook_, when he was a Captain of _Marines_, quarter'd at a Village where he buried a pretty many of his Men: At length the Parson refus'd to perform the Ceremony of their Internment any more, unless he was paid for it, which being told Captain _Rook_,

he ordered Six Men of his Company to carry the Corpse of the Soldier, then dead, and lay him upon the Parson's Hall-Table. This so embarass'd the Parson, that he sent the Captain Word, _If he'd fetch the Man away, he'd bury him and his whole Company for nothing_.

192. A reverend and charitable Divine, for the Benefit of the Country where he resided, caused a large Causeway to be begun: As he was one Day overlooking the Work, a certain Nobleman came by, _Well_, Doctor, says he, _for all your great Pains and Charity, I don't take this to be the Highway to Heaven: Very true, my Lord_, replied the Doctor, _for if it had, I shou'd have wondered to have met your Lordship here_.

193. Two Jesuits having pack'd together an innumerable Parcel of miraculous Lies, a Person who heard them, without taking upon him to contradict them, told 'em one of his own: That at St. _Alban_'s, there was a Stone Cistern, in which Water was always preserv'd for the Use of that Saint; and that ever since, if a Swine shou'd eat out of it, he wou'd instantly die: The Jesuits, hugging themselves at the Story, set out the next Day to St. _Alban_'s, where they found themselves miserably deceived: On their Return, they upbraided the Person with telling them so monstrous a Story; _Look ye there now_, said he, _you

told me a hundred Lies t'other Night, and I had more Breeding than to contradict you, I told you but one, and you have rid twenty Miles to confute me, which is very uncivil_.

194. A _Welchman_ and an _Englishman_ vapouring one Day at the Fruitfulness of their Countries; the _Englishman_ said, there was a Close near the Town where he was born, which was so fertile, that if a _Kiboo_ was thrown in over Night, it would be so cover'd with Grass, that 'twould be difficult to find it the next Day; _Splut_, says the _Welchman, what's that_? _There's a Close where hur was born, where you may put your Horse in over Night, and not be able to find him next Morning._

195. A Country Fellow in King _Charles_ the IId's. Time, selling his Load of Hay in the _Haymarket_, two Gentlemen who came out of the _Blue-Posts_, were talking of Affairs; one said, that Things did not go right, the King had been at the House and prorogued the Parliament. The Countryman coming Home, was ask'd what News in _London_? _Odsheart_, says he, _there's something to do there; the King, it seems, has_ berogued _the Parliament sadly_.

196. A wild young Gentleman having married a very discreet, virtuous young Lady; the better to reclaim him, she caused it to be given out at his Return, that she was dead, and had been buried: In the mean Time, she had so plac'd herself in Disguise, as to be able to observe how he took the News; and finding him still the same gay inconstant Man he always had been, she appear'd to him as the Ghost of herself, at which he seemed not at all dismay'd: At length disclosing herself to him, he then appear'd pretty much surpriz'd: a Person by said, _Why, Sir, you seem more afraid now than before; Ay_, replied he, _most Men are more afraid of a living Wife, than a dead one_.

197. An under Officer of the Customs at the Port of _Liverpool_, running heedlessly along a Ship's Gunnel, happened to tip over-board, and was drown'd; being soon after taken up, the Coroner's Jury was summoned to sit upon the Body. One of the Jury-Men returning home, was call'd to by an Alderman of the Town, and ask'd what Verdict they brought in, and whether they found it _Felo de se: Ay, ay_, says the Jury-Man shaking his Noddle, _he fell into the Sea, sure enough_.

198. One losing a Bag of Money of about 50_l._ between _Temple-Gate_

and _Temple-Bar_, fix'd a Paper up, offering 10_l._ Reward to those who took it up, and should return it: Upon which the Person that had it came and writ underneath to the following Effect, _Sir, I thank you, but you bid me to my Loss_.

199. Two brothers coming to be executed once for some enormous Crime; the Eldest was first turn'd off, without saying one Word: The other mounting the Ladder, began to harangue the Crowd, whose Ears were attentively open to hear him, expecting some Confession from him, _Good People_, says he, _my Brother hangs before my Face, and you see what a lamentable_ Spectacle _he makes; in a few Moments, I shall be turned off too, and then you'll see a Pair of_ Spectacles.

200. It was an usual saying of King _Charles_ II. _That Sailors get their Money like Horses, and spent it like Asses_; the following Story is somewhat an instance of it: One Sailor coming to see another on Pay-day, desired to borrow twenty Shillings of him; the money'd Man fell to telling out the Sum in Shillings, but a Half-Crown thrusting its Head in, put him out, and he began to tell again, but then an impertinent Crown-piece was as officious as it's half Brother had been,

and again interrupted the Tale; so that taking up a Handful of Silver, he cry'd, _Here_, Jack, _give me a Handful when your Ship's paid, what a Pox signifies counting it_.

201. A Person enquiring what became of _such a One_? _Oh! dear_, says one of the Company, _poor fellow, he dy'd insolvent, and was buried by the Parish: Died in solvent_, crys another, _that's a Lie, for he died in_ England, _I'm sure I was at his Burying_.

202. A humorous Countryman having bought a Barn, in Partnership with a Neighbour of his, neglected to make the least Use of it, whilst the other had plentifully stor'd his Part with Corn and Hay: In a little Time the latter came to him, and conscientiousily expostulated with him upon laying out his Money so fruitlessly: _Pray Neighbour_, says he, _ne'er trouble your Head, you may do what you will with your Part of the Barn, but I'll set mine o' Fire_.

203. An _Irishman_ whom King _Charles_ II. had some Esteem for, being only an inferior Servant of the Household, one Day coming into the King's Presence, his Majesty ask'd him how his Wife did, who had just before been cut for a _Fistula_ in her Backside. _I humbly thank your

Majesty_, replied Teague, _she's like to do well, but the Surgeon says, it will be an Eye-Sore as long as she lives_.

204. A young Gentlewoman who had married a very wild Spark, that had run through a plentiful Fortune, and was reduced to some Streights, was innocently saying to him one Day, _My Dear, I want some Shifts sadly_. _Shifts, Madam_, replies he, _D---- me, how can that be, when we make so many every Day?_

205. A Fellow once standing in the Pillory at _Temple-Bar_, it occasioned a Stop, so that a Carman with a Load of Cheeses had much ado to pass, and driving just up to the Pillory, he asked what that was that was writ over the Person's Head: They told him, it was a Paper to signify his Crime, that he stood for _Forgery_: Ay, says he, what is _Forgery_? They answered him, that _Forgery_ was counterfeiting another's Hand, with Intent to cheat People: To which the Carman replied, looking up at the Offender, Ah, Pox! this comes of your Writing and Reading, you silly Dog.

206. Master _Johnny_ sitting one Summer's Evening on the Green with his Mother's Chamber-maid, among other little Familiarities, as kissing,

pressing her Bubbies and the like, took the Liberty unawares to satisfy himself whereabouts she ty'd her Garters, and by an unlucky Slip went farther than he should have done: At which the poor Creature blushing, cry'd, _Be quiet, Mr._ John, _I'll throw this Stone at your Head, else_. _Ay, Child_, says he, _and I'll fling two at your Tail if you do_.

207. When the Prince of _Orange_ came over, Five of the Seven Bishops who were sent to the Tower declar'd for his Highness, and the other Two would not come into Measures; upon which Mr. _Dryden_ said, _that the_
seven Golden Candlesticks _were sent to be essay'd in the_ Tower, _and five of them prov'd_ Prince'_s Metal_.

208. A Dog coming open-mouth'd at a Serjeant upon a March, he run the Spear of his Halbert into his Throat and kill'd him: The Owner coming out rav'd extreamly that his Dog was kill'd, and ask'd the Serjeant, _Why, he could not as well have struck at him with the blunt End of his Halbert?_ _So I would_, says he, _if he had run at me with his Tail_.

209. King Charles the IId. being in Company with the Lord _Rochester_, and others of the Nobility, who had been drinking the best Part of the

Night, _Killegrew_ came in; Now, says the King, we shall hear of our Faults: _No, Faith_, says _Killegrew, I don't care to trouble my Head with that which all the Town talks of_.

210. A rich old Miser finding himself very ill, sent for a Parson to administer the last Consolation of the Church to him: Whilst the Ceremony was performing, old _Gripewell_ falls into a Fit; on his Recovery the Doctor offered the Chalice to him; _Indeed_, crys he, _I can't afford to lend you above twenty Shillings upon't, I can't upon my Word_.

211. A Person who had a chargeable Stomach, used often to asswage his Hunger at a Lady's Table, having one Time or other promis'd to help her to a Husband. At length he came to her, _Now Madam_, says he, _I have brought you a Knight, a Man of Worship and Dignity, one that will furnish out a Table well_. _Phoo_, says the Lady, _your Mind's ever running on your Belly_; _No_, says he, _'tis sometimes running o'yours you see_.

212. One, who had been a very termagant Wife, lying on her Death-bed, desired her Husband, _That as she had brought him a Fortune she might

have Liberty to make her Will, for bestowing a few Legacies to her Relations: No, by G--d, Madam_, says he, _You had your Will, all your Life-time, and now I'll have mine_.

213. When the Lord _Jefferies_, before he was a Judge, was pleading at the Bar once, a Country Fellow giving Evidence against his Client, push'd the Matter very home on the Side he swore of; _Jefferies_, after his usual Way, call'd out to the Fellow, _Hark you, you Fellow in the Leather-Doublet, what have you for swearing?_ To which the Countryman smartly reply'd, _Faith, Sir, if you have no more for Lying than I have for Swearing, you may go in a Leather Doublet too_.

214. The same _Jefferies_ afterwards on the Bench, told an old Fellow with a long Beard, that _he supposed he had a Conscience as long as his Beard: Does your Lordship_, replies the old Man, _measure Consciences by Beards? if so, your Lordship has no Beard at all._

215. _Apelles_, the famous Painter, having drawn the Picture of _Alexander_ the Great on Horseback, brought it and presented it to that Prince, but he not bestowing that Praise on it, which so excellent a Piece deserv'd, _Apelles_ desired a living Horse might be brought; who

mov'd by Nature fell a prancing and neighing, as tho' it had actually been his living Fellow-Creature; whereupon _Apelles_ told _Alexander, his Horse understood Painting better than himself_.

216. An old Gentleman who had married a fine young Lady, and being terribly afraid of Cuckoldom, took her to Task one Day, and ask'd her, if she had considered what a crying Sin it was in a Woman to cuckold her Husband? _Lord, my Dear_, says she, _what d'ye mean? I never had such a Thought in my Head, nor never will_: _No, no_, replied he, _I shall have it in my Head, you'll have it some where else_.

217. The late Lord _Dorset_, in a former Reign, was asking a certain Bishop, _why he conferr'd Orders on so many Blockheads_. _Oh, my Lord_, says he, 'tis better the Ground should be plowed _by Asses, than lie quite untill'd_.

218. A certain Lady, to excuse herself for a Frailty she had lately fallen into, said to an intimate Friend of hers, _Lord, how is it possible for a Woman to keep her Cabinet unpickt, when every Fellow has got a Key to it_.

219. Mr. _Dryden_, once at Dinner, being offered by a Lady the Rump of a Fowl, and refusing it, the Lady said, Pray, Mr. _Dryden_, take it, the Rump is the best Part of the _Fowl_; Yes, Madam, says he, and so I think it is of the _Fair_.

220. A Company of Gamesters falling out at a Tavern, gave one another very scurvy Language: At length those dreadful Messengers of Anger, the Bottles and Glasses flew about like Hail-Shot; one of which mistaking it's Errand, and hitting the Wainscot, instead of the Person's Head it was thrown at, brought the Drawer rushing in, who cry'd, _D'ye call Gentlemen?_ _Call Gentlemen_, says one of the Standers by; _no they don't call_ Gentlemen, _but they call one another_ Rogue _and_ Rascal, _as fast as they can_.

221. An amorous young Fellow making very warm Addresses to a marry'd Woman, _Pray, Sir, be quiet_, said she, _I have a Husband that won't thank you for making him a Cuckold_: _No Madam_, reply'd he, _but you will I hope_.

222. One observing a crooked Fellow in close Argument with another, who would have dissuaded him from some inconsiderable Resolution; said to

his Friend, _Prithee, let him alone, and say no more to him, you see he's_ bent _upon it_.

223. Bully _Dawson_ was overturned in a Hackney-Coach once, pretty near his Lodgings, and being got on his Legs again, he said, 'Twas the greatest Piece of Providence that ever befel him, for it had saved him the Trouble of bilking the Coachman.

224. A vigorous young Officer, who made Love to a Widow, coming a little unawares upon her once, caught her fast in his Arms. _Hey day_, say she, _what do you fight after the_ French _Way: take Towns before you declare War?_ No, faith, Widow says he, but I should be glad to imitate them so far, to be in the Middle of the Country before you could resist me.

225. Sir _Godfrey Kneller_, and the late Dr. _Ratcliffe_, had a Garden in common, but with one Gate: Sir _Godfrey_, upon some Occasion, ordered the Gate to be nail'd up; when the Doctor heard of it, he said, _He did not Care what Sir_ Godfrey _did to the Gate, so he did not paint it_. This being told Sir _Godfrey_, he replied, _He would take that, or any Thing from his good Friend, the Doctor, but his Physick_.

226. The same Physician, who was not the humblest Man in the World, being sent for by Sir _Edward Seymour_, who was said to be the proudest; the Knight received him, while he was dressing his Feet and picking his Toes, being at that Time troubled with a _Diabetis_, and upon the Doctor's entering the Room, accosted him in this Manner, _So Quack_, said he, _I'm a dead Man, for I piss sweet_; _Do ye_, replied the Doctor, _then prithee piss upon your Toes, for they stink damnably_: And so turning round on his Heel went out of the Room.

227. A certain worthy Gentleman having among his Friends the Nickname of _Bos_, which was a Kind of Contraction of his real Name, when his late Majesty conferred the Honour of Peerage upon him, a Pamphlet was soon after published with many sarcastical Jokes upon him, and had this Part of a Line from _Horace_ as a Motto, _viz._

    ----_Optat Ephippia Bos_----

My Lord asked a Friend, who could read _Latin_, what that meant? It is as much as to say, my Lord, said he, that you become _Honours as a Sow does a Saddle_. O! very fine, said my Lord: Soon after another Friend coming to see him, the Pamphlet was again spoken of, I would, said my Lord, give five hundred Pounds to know the Author of it. I don't know the Author of the Pamphlet, said his Friend, but I know who wrote the Motto; Ay, cry'd my Lord, _prithee who was it? Horace_, answered the other: _How_, replied his Lordship, _a dirty Dog, that his Return for all the Favours I have done him and his Brother_.

228. A wild Gentleman having pick'd up his own Wife for a Mistress, the Man, to keep his Master in Countenance, got to Bed to the Maid too. In the Morning, when the Thing was discovered, the Fellow was obliged, in Attonement for his Offence, to make the Girl amends by marrying her; _Well_, says he, _little did my Master and I think last Night, that we were robbing our own Orchards_.

229. One seeing a kept Whore, who made a very great Figure, ask'd, what Estate she had? _Oh_, says another, _a very good Estate in_ Tail.

230. In the great Dispute between _South_ and _Sherlock_, the former, who was a great Courtier, said, His Adversary reasoned well, but he Bark'd like a Cur: To which the other reply'd, That Fawning was the Property of a Cur, as well as Barking.

231. Second Thoughts, we commonly say, are best; and young Women who pretend to be averse to Marriage, desire not to be taken at their Words. One asking a Girl, _if she would have him?_ _Faith, no_, John, says she, _but you may have me if you will_.

232. A Gentleman lying on his Death-Bed, called to his Coachman, who had been an old Servant, and said, _Ah!_ Tom, _I'm going a long rugged Journey, worse than ever you drove me?_ Oh, dear Sir_, reply'd the Fellow (he having been but an indifferent Master to him), _ne'er let that discourage you, for it is all down Hill_.

233. An honest bluff Country Farmer, meeting the Parson of the Parish in a By-Lane, and not giving him the Way so readily as he expected, the Parson, with an erected Crest, told him, _He was better fed than taught: Very likely indeed Sir_, reply'd the Farmer: _For you teach me and I feed myself_.

234. A famous Teacher of _Arithmetick_, who had long been married without being able to get his Wife with Child: One said to her, Madam, your Husband is an excellent _Arithmetician_. Yes, replies she, only he

can't _multiply_.

235. One making a furious Assault upon a hot Apple-pye, burnt his Mouth 'till the Tears ran down; his Friend asked him, _Why he wept?_ _Only_, says he, _'tis just come into my Mind, that my Grand-mother dy'd this Day twelvemonth_: _Phoo!_ says the other, _is that all?_ So whipping a large Piece into his Mouth, he quickly sympathiz'd with his Companion; who seeing his Eyes brim full, with a malicious Sneer ask'd him, _why he wept?_ _A Pox on you_, says he, _because you were not hanged the same Day your Grand-mother dy'd_.

236. A Lady who had married a Gentleman that was a tolerable Poet, one Day sitting alone with him, she said, Come, my Dear, you write upon other People, prithee write something for me; let me see what Epitaph you'll bestow upon me when I die: Oh, my Dear, reply'd he, that's a melancholy Subject, prithee don't think of it: Nay, upon my Life you shall, adds she,----Come, I'll begin,

----_Here lies_ Bidd:

To which he answer'd, _Ah! I wish she did_.

237. A Cowardly Servant having been hunting with his Lord, they had kill'd a wild Boar; the Fellow seeing the Boar stir, betook himself to a Tree; upon which his Master call'd to him, and asked him, _what he was afraid of the Boar's Gut's were out?_ _No matter for that_, says he, _his Teeth are in_.

238. One telling another that he had once so excellent a Gun that it went off immediately upon a Thief's coming into the House, altho' it wasn't charged: _How the Devil can that be?_ said t'other: _Because_, said the First, _the Thief_ carry'd _it off, and what was worse, before I had Time to_ charge _him with it_.

239. Some Gentlemen coming out of a Tavern pretty merry, a Link-Boy cry'd, _Have a Light, Gentlemen?_ _Light yourself to the Devil, you Dog_, says one of the Company: _Bless you, Master_, reply'd the Boy, _we can find the Way in the Dark; shall we light your Worship thither_.

240. A Person was once try'd at _Kingston_ before the late Lord Chief Justice _Holt_, for having two Wives, where one _Unit_ was to have been the chief Evidence against him: After much calling for him, Word was

brought that they could hear nothing of him. _No_, says his Lordship, _why then, all I can say, is, Mr._ Unit _stands for a_ Cypher.

241. 'Tis certainly the most transcendent Pleasure to be agreeably surpriz'd with the Confession of Love, from an ador'd Mistress. A young Gentleman, after a very great Misfortune came to his Mistress, and told her, He was reduc'd even to the want of five Guineas: To which she replied, _I am glad of it with all my Heart_: Are you so, Madam, adds he, suspecting her Constancy: Pray, why so? _Because_, says she, _I can furnish you with five Thousand_.

242. On a Publick Night of Rejoicing, when Bonefires and Illuminations were made, some honest Fellows were drinking the King's Health and Prosperity to _England, as long as the Sun and Moon endured_: Ay, says one, and 500 Years after, _for I have put both my Sons Apprentices to a Tallow-Chandler_.

243. A young Fellow who had made an End of all he had, even to his last Suit of Cloathes; one said to him, Now I hope, you'll own yourself a happy Man, for you have made an End of all your Cares: How so, said the Gentleman; _Because_, said the other, _you've nothing left to take care

of _.

244. Some years ago, when his Majesty used to hunt frequently in _Richmond-Park_, it brought such Crowds of People thither, that Orders were given to admit none, when the King was there himself, but the Servants of the Household. A fat Country Parson having, on one of these Days a strong Inclination to make one of the Company, Captain _B-d-ns_, promised to introduce him, but coming to the Gate, the Keepers would have stopp'd him, by telling him, none but the Houshold were to be admitted: Why, d--mn you, said the Captain, don't you know the Gentleman? _He's his Majesty's Hunting-Chaplain_: Upon which the Keepers asked Pardon, and left the reverend Gentleman to Recreation.

245. The learned Mr. _Charles Barnard_, Serjeant Surgeon to Queen _Anne_, being very severe upon _Parsons_ having _Pluralities_. A reverend and worthy Divine heard him a good while with Patience, but at length took him up with this Question, _Why do you Mr. Serjeant_ Barnard _rail thus at_ Pluralities, _who have always so many_ Sine-Cures _upon your own Hands_?

246. Dr. _Lloyd_, Bishop of _Worcester_, so eminent for his

Prophesies, when by his Sollicitations and Compliance at Court, he got removed from a poor _Welch_ Bishoprick to a rich _English_ one. A reverend Dean of the Church said, _That he found his Brother_ Lloyd _spelt Prophet with an_ F[2].

[2] Most of the Clergy follow this Spelling.

247. A worthy old Gentleman in the Country, having employ'd an Attorney, of whom he had a pretty good Opinion, to do some Law Business for him in _London_, he was greatly surprized on his coming to Town, and demanding his Bill of Law Charges, to find that it amounted to at least three Times the Sum he expected; the honest Attorney assured him, that there was no Article in his Bill, but what was _fair and reasonable_: Nay, said the Country Gentleman, here is one of them I am sure cannot be so, for you have set down three Shillings and four Pence for going to _Southwark_, when none of my Business lay that Way; pray what is the Meaning of that Sir; _Oh! Sir_, said he, _that was for fetching the_ Chine _and_ Turkey _from the Carriers, that you sent me for a_ Present, _out of the Country_.

FINIS.

Project Gutenberg

Made in the USA
Middletown, DE
27 March 2017